The Inward Sun

7 Practices to engage, aspire, achieve

by David M. Castro

First Arch Street Press edition November 25, 2019

ARCH STREET PRESS, ARCH ST. PRESS
and colophon are registered trademarks of Arch Street Press.

For information about special discounts for bulk and nonprofit purchases,
please contact Arch Street Press: sales@archstreetpress.org.

Book design by idesign communications
Cover design by idesign communications

Library of Congress Cataloging-in-Publication Data is available.

ISBN: 978-1-938798-27-6
ISBN: 978-1-938798-28-3 (e-book)

Dedication

For Julia, the love and lion of my life.

Contents

Acknowledgments   vii

About the Title   ix

Preface   xi

Introduction   xv
  Domains and Practices   1

First Domain: Engaging   5
  Mindfulness: Breathing Meditation   8
  Mindfulness: Observe Your Impulsive Mind   9
  Mindfulness: Observe Your Stress Response   11
  Compassion: Listening Practice   12
  Compassion: Identity Molecule   13
  Compassion: The Left-Hand Column   15
  Compassion: Compassion Meditation   17
  Compassion: Tonglen   19

Second Domain: Aspiring   21
  Vision: Journaling Your Vision and Values   24
  Visioning: Connecting and Reconnecting with Your Vision
  and Values   26
  Willpower: Personal Visualization–I Want, I Will, I Won't   27
  Willpower: Self-Mastery–Surfing the Urge   30
  Resilience: Pause and Plan   32
  Resilience: Self-Forgiveness, Gratitude and Self-Care   34

Third Domain: Achieving   37
  Dynamics: Courage, Concentration and Peak Performance   41
  Dynamics: Framing Visions and Values as Dynamic Variables   43

Dynamics: Observing Dynamic Relationships Connected to
Visions and Values   45
Genership: Surfacing Mental Models, Interests and Visions   47
Genership: Seeking Help for Our Visions and Interests   49
Genership: Benevolent, Constructive Engagement   51
Genership: Collaborative Participation in Circles of Practice   52

Next Steps: From Base Camp to the Tree Line   53

Acknowledgments

I want to acknowledge my close colleagues at I-LEAD and Arch Street Press, who spent many days in patient conversations with me as this book was taking shape, offering thoughts and revisions, and most importantly, helping me conceptualize and clearly express these practices based on our many years of work together serving communities. Special thanks to Ann Black, Cynda Clyde, Cheryl Lang, Angel Figueroa, Phillip Thomas, Barbara Wilkinson-Sykes and Robert Rimm. I also want to express gratitude to my friends at Radnor Quaker Meeting, and to Pamela Boyce Simms for essential spiritual guidance on this journey.

About the Title

As our team was putting the finishing touches on the layout and graphics for this book, I took a trip to Ecuador with my youngest son, Fernando. Our plan was to spend three weeks studying Spanish and also exploring parts of the Andes mountains in Ecuador. We succeeded in having an amazing journey.

I am an active Quaker, and so, in my preparation for this trip, I made contact with Quakers in Ecuador. I discovered a small but active Quaker meeting in our homebase city of Quito. The Quakers I met there were warm and welcoming, especially former Ambassador Andrew Winter and his wife, Maria Isabel. They helped us with our travel plans, met with us, and invited us into their lives and homes for meals and fellowship. Due to our adventures and their meeting schedules, we were not able to share a meeting for worship with the Quito Quakers until the Sunday that we were scheduled to return to the United States.

As you may know, Quakers practice a form of deeply meditative silent worship in which individuals only speak in the meeting when they feel inspired by God with a spiritual message for those gathered. Meetings generally include long periods of silence with only a few powerful messages that are spoken into that special space reserved for quiet group reflection on spiritual matters. In the Quaker meeting that Sunday, I met the Quito group organizer, Jorge Arauz, with whom I had a wonderful encounter before the meeting. An Ecuador native and professional counselor and psychologist, Jorge had spent many years in Philadelphia near where I am based in the United States. We discovered many shared connections among people, places and organizations. Jorge has a profound spiritual presence that I have observed over the years with many Quakers, and I sensed that the meeting for worship would be very special.

Within the small and intimate meeting for worship, Jorge offered a spiritual message that greatly inspired me. Although I cannot capture his message verbatim, I will try my best to relay its spiritual substance. Jorge began by commenting on the old gospel song, "This Little Light of Mine." He said that adults mistakenly and, perhaps with a touch of hubris, think of the spiritual light within children as a "little" light. "No," said Jorge, "the light within children is not little. It is an awesome, powerful, inspiring light. A light to guide the world." Then Jorge talked about the powerful light from the sun, the starlight that warms us and is the source of all life on Earth. He said that in addition to this outward light, this powerful sunlight, each of us has within us another corresponding light, an "inward sun." And through the spiritual light of this powerful inward sun, we can choose love, choose peace, choose trust, choose faith. The inward sun is even brighter and more powerful than the sun in our sky.

Jorge's profound spiritual message resonated deeply with me that morning. *The Inward Sun.* I knew that I had found the title for this book. Because the inward sun is what the Seven Practices help us find. Our inward spiritual sun provides the energy through which we engage, aspire and achieve as spiritual beings. The other metaphor that I have often used in this book involves climbing the mountain together. Remember, we do so to experience and celebrate the inward and outward sun reflected on the world that we are creating. Thank you, Quito Quakers. Thank you, Jorge!

Preface

If you have opened these pages, you probably have a desire to change yourself or the world around you. Because you are part of the world, to change yourself is a way of beginning to undertake more ambitious change projects. You are alive, and change is what life does. An essential characteristic of all life and living systems is to engage in a process of creatively transforming the world. Beginning as a seed, a tree transforms light, soil, air and water into a living structure of branches and leaves. Sentient creatures transform air, food and water into their complex flesh, bones and blood. Through the biochemical exchange across its cellular membrane, even the smallest bacterium is busy coherently organizing the world that surrounds it. Through its evolving forms and patterns, life asserts its inner light, its creative vision upon the animate and inanimate universe that surrounds it. The presence of this intentional, organizing, transforming, creative capacity is exactly how we know that something is alive.

In human nature, we find the greatest concentration of creative, transformative power on earth. Our inward sun creates enormous responsibility and risk, because change entails not only the power to create, but also to destroy. Change also presents the potential for unintended consequences, wherein we may set out to support life but end up damaging it, often with painful results.

As a leadership teacher and practitioner, I have spent my professional life helping individuals and organizations enhance their creative powers, so that they become better at this essential challenge of change. I have helped leaders expand their vision, become more intentional and efficient in their actions, avoid unintended consequences, achieve success and joy for themselves and others, and bounce back from failures and difficulties. This book draws from my two decades of experience in this work.

More than 10 years ago, I wrote my first book about creativity and leadership, entitled *Genership: Beyond Leadership Toward Liberating the Creative Soul*. In *Genership*, I provided a conceptual and philosophical account explaining that creativity is the most essential facet of human nature and that the ability to create with others is the most important skill for individuals and organizations. Genership is the word I use to describe this capacity. Ideas about human creativity that I develop within the book involve the limitations of science, knowledge and rationality. I also explore the tension and distinction between reflective thought—involving understanding, description and necessary prediction—versus creativity, involving intentional change emerging from creative vision. A fundamental insight is that we cannot study our way to creativity and change. To understand or know something it must first exist. But creativity and change is about what does *not* yet exist. For this reason, creativity is always on the frontier of rational knowledge and understanding. *Genership* provides a guide to the functioning of creativity in groups, with an emphasis on understanding rather than practice.

The Inward Sun, in contrast to *Genership*, emphasizes practice and action rather than reflection and understanding.

Many years of self-development and work with others have helped me learn that increasing our creative power requires practicing skills as well as increasing knowledge and understanding. The creative limitation on rational understanding is that it initially presents in a reflective mode. As I explore in *Genership*, the fundamental human capacity to reason involves holding the mirror of our consciousness up to nature. This mimetic quality of reason provides a gateway to transformation, but the actual work of creativity requires more. Rationality does not manifest as creative change without adding intentional action. Acquiring knowledge—especially "book" knowledge—is essentially a reflective activity. I can read about meditation to understand what it is. But until I sit in a chair and close my eyes to practice meditation, it will remain an abstraction. I can study the recommendations made by various experts to achieve high-functioning teams. But I won't know what works in any particular organization until I create such a team in practice. Most importantly, the practice of meditation and developing teams will always entail insights and abilities that are unknowable and unworkable without having participated in them as living, creative actions.

On the other hand, action can, and often does, bring about change irrespective of grounding in learning or understanding. The changes associated with evolution have been proceeding for millenia without capture within a rational framework. Sometimes we are lucky and what we do without clear intention or insight works for us. We may survive and even prosper for a time without understanding what works and why. Without penetrating understanding, however, our luck eventually runs out. Then, what once worked ceases to function, often leading to frustration, failure and even tragedy.

For our lives and communities to thrive, we must combine understanding with the development of robust skills that evolve into coherent, adaptable practices. During my career helping empower leaders and changemakers (including myself), I have realized that the precious ability to navigate this transition from thought to action to evolving practice is really how individuals and organizations succeed. To *know* is not the same as *to do*. *To do* is not the same as *to do well*. *To do well* is not the same as *to do better*, improving over a long time span. Failure occurs when people cannot successfully navigate these transitions.

The secret to reconciling reflective thought and successful action is practice, where knowledge manifests as effective action, where ideas grapple with reality and find purchase. Practice is why humanity has continued to thrive. Our shared future depends on becoming better and stronger at practice and practical knowledge.

In this book, *The Inward Sun*, I offer a coherent set of foundational practices that you can implement in your life, and that a team can use within an organization, to become consistent changemakers able to manifest creative, healthy and sustainable change. In this context, think of creativity as the intentional changes that you want to see in yourself and the world.

Each of us who answers life's call to creative collaboration experiences different outcomes. Some will experience frustration and failure; some, stress and unhappiness; some, enthusiasm and joy. And some will experience meaning and satisfaction. The practices advanced in this book are designed to increase your sense of meaning, joy and satisfaction as you collaborate with others to create what you and your community envision for both the present moment and the future.

These practices will help you to express your inward sun, create what you want for yourself and those you love as you live in the world, so that you can realize your life's unique potential. Your life is not written in thoughts and words. It is written in the language of action. What you do is what really matters. Think of these practices as a vocabulary of action to help your insights and understandings take flight.

Introduction

Daybreak at Basecamp

Many years ago as part of a leadership-development experience, I climbed a mountain with a group of 10 men and women in Colorado. Early in the morning, our team gathered at a base camp at the bottom of the mountain to prepare for the adventure. We imagined ourselves standing in the sunshine on the mountaintop, and what kind of internal energy we would need to get there.

We were excited, filled with anticipation. We were also concerned. Did we have the right clothing and tools? Did we have the skills to meet the challenges we would face as we scrambled up steep slopes and crawled over seemingly vertical fields of boulders? Did we have the stamina to make it all the way to the summit? Would we experience injury or altitude sickness? Many of us weren't in terrific physical shape and, having come from coastal areas, were feeling lightheaded in the thin air. The trip to the summit would take two days, requiring camping overnight in tents. Were we prepared to spend a night sleeping outdoors in a frozen wilderness?

As part of my preparation for that day, I read some books and articles on mountain climbing. Not everyone on the team had engaged in such preparation. As we started our climb, I noted that my book knowledge about climbing was just about useless. In some cases it was a hindrance as I continually had to manage the differences between my imagined expectations and our actual experiences. For example, I had read that it would get colder as we made our ascent. But none of the authors mentioned that the worst cold was early in the morning simply from the lack of sun and physical activity. That morning we had to kindle both the external and internal fire for the challenge ahead. Those who were less prepared were actually doing better in some situations because they were able to be fully present to their experience, rather than distracted by comparing their expectations to reality.

In the years since this adventure (yes, we made it to the top), my experience climbing a mountain in Colorado has served as an ever-present reminder that *knowing* about something is nothing like *doing* it. Our world is filled with armchair experts: people with knowledge gained from reading, watching and listening, but who lack direct experience. If you have ever tried to do something based on what you heard or read, you will immediately understand the limitations of "armchair" expertise.

Observing an activity or process can provide some insights about how it works, but the actual experience of trying it ourselves creates a deeper vein of understanding and insight. Through participatory experience we become entangled with that which we attempt to understand. On the field of action and participation we transcend observation, collapsing the distance between subject and object, producing more profound understanding and mastery by becoming one with the world.

This book aspires to help you approach your personal empowerment and that of your chosen community through the path of the practitioner, the doer, the one who engages, acts and becomes one with the world.

Our goal is not to help you *think* about these practices but to consistently *do* them. Our focus is on helping you climb the mountain. We do offer you resources for a time when you may want to rest, reflect and understand more deeply. Through our online community at www.i-lead.social, we have referred you to what we believe are seminal works that will help you understand these practices within a historical, scientific, cultural, psychological and religious framework. But remember that the philosopher of mountain climbing and the one who climbs mountains are not necessarily the same person with the same experiences. If you want to reach the top of a mountain, the doer may well be more helpful to you than the knower.

What happens when you cease trying to understand in the abstract, get out of your chair, get onto the field of action, out into the arena and fully engage? How can you do that? Only by putting on your backpack and setting out on the path. Find your inward sun and start climbing!

Domains and Practices

The activities, behaviors and practices that we describe here fall within three Domains of Action: Engaging, Aspiring and Achieving. We describe each Domain and its attendant practices more fully below. Understanding the Seven Practices through the lens of these Domains will help you fully develop your strengths and skills.

Within the Domains of Action, the practices are developmental and interrelate dynamically. Engagement provides the foundation for aspiration and, in turn, aspiration leads to achievement. Mindfulness and compassion lead to visioning, visioning leads to willpower and resilience, and together this group of practices informs dynamics and genership. Most of the personal and organizational difficulties that we experience in the world today arise from weak fundamental practices and inadequate development across the Domains.

As you master these practices, you will discover that they are deeply connected to your spirit and that of your community. As a conscious, living being you are aware of your presence in the stream of time and change. You may also be aware that you are constantly moving and changing and that your change and motion are connected to the energy in the universe that began at the dawn of time and that will continue on through eternity. You are your inward sun, a pattern of energy that belongs to this universe. You are the light from that inward star and you are connected to the light that was present at the dawn of creation. The practices we describe in this book will help you to become connected to your inner spiritual energy, to see and respond to that energy in others, to master and channel this energy, and to combine your energy creatively with others so that you can live out your deepest potential and that of your chosen community.

First Domain – Engaging

Engaging refers to your ability to become awake to your inward sun: what is going on inside your mind, heart and body. It also includes engagement with others and with the natural and man-made world. To what extent are you open to and aware of your thoughts, feelings, emotions and bodily sensations? To what extent are you open to and aware of these experiences in others? To what extent are you able to observe and comprehend the context and dynamics within which you exist and conduct your activities?

The Domain of Engagement builds upon two practices: *Mindfulness* and *Compassion*.

Mindfulness practices increase your awareness of yourself, others and the world without judgment. Mindfulness practices teach you how to maintain your focus on the present moment without compromise from internal or external distractions.

Compassion practices help you to direct your inward sun, to develop loving interactions with yourself, others and the world. When you realize that you are unwell or suffering emotional pain, you are demonstrating mindfulness about yourself. When you help yourself heal, you are showing yourself compassion. When you become aware of another's suffering, you are practicing mindfulness. When you help that person relieve his or her suffering, you are practicing compassion.

Second Domain — Aspiring

Aspiring refers to your creative powers. As a human being, you have extraordinary agency. You can change yourself, others and the world around you. The Domain of Aspiring entails three core practices:

Vision, *Willpower* and *Resilience*.

Vision practices involve your ability to imagine in great detail what you desire and what you want to create with others. Willpower practices involve your ability to focus energy on moving your current reality toward your vision. Resilience practices involve your ability to learn from and persist in the face of obstacles and failures. For example, when you imagine yourself inventing a new medicine, you are practicing visioning. When you study biochemistry to develop this medicine, you are practicing willpower. When the prototype of your new medicine fails and you respond with learning and persistence, you are practicing resilience.

Third Domain — Achieving

Achieving entails two practices: *Dynamics* and *Genership.*

Dynamics involves your ability to work effectively with others to identify, map, track and relate key variables in your sphere of influence. The ideas of change and development require the presence of variables. Your ability to create change requires focus on qualities or quantities that are changeable, and therefore understood as variables. The Seventh Practice is Genership. This involves your ability to surface the interests and desires of others and work collaboratively to make mutual progress possible for everyone. Genership also involves your ability to form strong learning relationships and communities. When you assemble a team of players who practice together to win a championship, or a team of artists and engineers to collaborate on design, you are practicing in these arenas involving Dynamics along with Genership.

Genership represents the culmination and integration of all the other practices.

The Celtic Triquetra

First Domain: Engaging

Awareness is like the sun.
When it shines on things, they are transformed.

Thich Nhat Hanh

The First Domain

The First Domain of Action, Engaging, draws upon two practices: Mindfulness and Compassion.

Mindfulness is the practice of paying attention to what is happening internally and externally. Compassion is the practice of creating loving relationships with yourself and others.

Mindfulness
Within the practice of Mindfulness, there are three sub-practices:

- Mindfulness Breathing Meditation
- Observing Your Impulsive Mind
- Observing Your Stress Response

Breathing Meditation is designed to strengthen your ability to direct your focus.

Observing your Impulsive Mind and Observing Your Stress Response are practices designed to strengthen your ability to pay attention to the ways in which you may become distracted and suffer a loss of mindfulness.

These sub-practices are deceptively simple. They are difficult to put into action but provide significant pathways to personal empowerment when you work at them diligently—every day.

Compassion
The practice of Compassion includes five sub-practices:

- Listening
- Identity Molecule
- Left-Hand Column
- Compassion Meditation
- Tonglen

Listening practice is mindfulness diligently applied in dialogue with others. The Identity Molecule is a special form of mindfulness practice that focuses on self and other identity. Left-Hand Column is a form of mindfulness practice that focuses on what is said and left unsaid in dialogue. These three practices create a foundation for Compassion practice by deepening your awareness of others and of how you and others communicate and understand one another.

Compassion Meditation is a practice that strengthens your compassion "muscle"—both in terms of self-compassion and compassion for others.

Tonglen strengthens your ability to practice compassion in the face of anxiety and stress that may arise from fear, longing, pain and other related primal emotions. Generally, these are practices that you work on with others, on a daily basis.

Mindful listening for long periods without interruption is difficult to practice in normal conversation and encounters. For this reason, you can conduct this practice on a weekly basis with others who have importance to you, especially those with whom you are engaged or wish to be engaged in ongoing collaborative efforts.

Taken together, these sub-practices—Mindfulness and Compassion—combine to radically enhance and empower your ability to engage positively in your own life, with those around you and with the world in which you live.

The Musical Notation for Breath

Mindfulness: *Breathing Meditation*

The practice of Mindfulness Breathing Meditation is straightforward but also deeply challenging. It is easy to describe but very hard to do. This is a practice you can do alone or with others. The heart of the practice is to focus on your breath. Observe yourself taking in a breath, and then focus on the "outbreath" as you exhale. Try to do the practice for at least five minutes a day and try to work up to a total period of 20 minutes. When you excel at this practice, you may wish to expand the time to an hour or longer.

You will notice that your mind drifts away from your breath as you practice Mindfulness Breathing Meditation. This may happen again and again no matter how long you have engaged in the practice. Wandering is what minds do. When you catch your mind drifting, merely observe your thoughts and then gently return to focusing on your breath.

Do not worry about the reason for the practice or what you may gain from it. Simply do it to the best of your abilities.

Mindfulness Breathing Meditation can be practiced while you are sitting, standing, walking or engaged in any other activity as long as you are able to focus on your breath.

Step by Step

- Sit comfortably or engage in any activity that doesn't require too much conscious effort (e.g. walking a simple path).
- Focus on your outbreath.
- When your mind wanders, notice this (thinking) without judgment.
- Return to focus on your outbreath.
- Continue for at least 10 minutes.

Ourorboros (Snake Devouring Itself)

Mindfulness: *Observing Your Impulsive Mind*

The practice of Observing Your Impulsive Mind requires you to become aware that you have two forms of consciousness. Psychologists have referred to these as System One and System Two. System One is your more ancient, primal form of consciousness: vigilant, constantly scanning and observing the environment, looking for immediate opportunities and threats. It makes decisions and forms judgments quickly, aware of small changes in your environment. System One is instinctual and impulsive, tightly integrated with your emotions and feelings. It has close access to your primal motivations of anger, fear, love, desire, lust, greed, hatred and other powerful emotions. It allows you to react quickly without thinking too much about what is happening.

System Two, on the other hand, is the one you use for creativity and deep analytical thought: your higher consciousness. It reasons, masters complexity and engages in intentional, strategic action. System One is always operating in the background. System Two requires conscious deployment. You will find that you are able to run away from danger without spending too much time planning. However, you will never accidentally or unconsciously write a novel or build a company.

The goal of this Mindfulness practice is to regularly and intentionally engage System Two in observing the behavior of System One. Do not attempt to judge the behavior of System One as good or bad, as helpful or destructive. Just observe and understand how your impulsive mind is active and influencing your behavior.

Step by Step

- Notice when you have an urge to act impulsively. This is something that you may be doing or wish to be doing without conscious thought, planning or reflection. It may also be an urge or feeling arising spontaneously or automatically.
- Observe your impulse, without judgment. What triggers it? How does it feel? Where does it go to? How does it play out?

Stress Vortex

Mindfulness: *Observing Your Stress Response*

Increasing mindfulness requires that you practice Observing Your Stress Response. What happens to your mind and body when you sense an important threat or opportunity? Does your heart beat faster? Do you have trouble sleeping? Do you feel nervous? Do you feel energized? Do you feel a sense of concern or worry? Do you eat more or less? Does stress trigger any behaviors such as eating or use of substances to affect your emotions? Does stress affect your patience, focus or emotional intensity? The essence of this practice is to note without judgment how you respond as your stress level increases. Within this practice, do not attempt to control your stress response. Just note how you respond mentally and physically when you feel pressure.

Step by Step

- Notice what you think, feel and do when you are feeling pressure or stress, without judgment.
- Ask yourself these questions: What thoughts come into your mind when you are under stress? What feelings arise during periods of stress? Do they manifest in any physical sensations? Do your thoughts and feelings cause you to undertake any impulsive behaviors? If so, how would you describe their nature, duration and character?

Hourglass

Compassion: *Listening Practice*

This basic Listening practice is performed with one other person. The instructions are simple: Listen intently to another person—for instance, a friend, colleague or family member—for eight minutes without interrupting, without asking questions, and completely letting go of your body language, agenda and critical judgment. Relax your interests, desires, expressions and requests for clarification. Relax your inclination to agree or disagree, to judge or classify what you are hearing as right or wrong, good or bad, worthy or unworthy. Just listen deeply and completely. At the end of eight minutes, if your partner is willing to listen in return, speak for eight minutes similarly without any interruptions, questions, guidance, feedback or critical judgment from your partner. Framing open-ended questions are optional, such as: What is happening in your life? What do you want for your life? What is concerning you right now? What do you observe at this time? What is your life story?

Step by Step

- Commit to listen deeply to your partner for a period of eight minutes.
- Commit not to ask questions.
- Commit not to interrupt.
- Commit not to direct the flow of communication that you are receiving through facial expressions or any other physical gestures.
- Give your complete focus.
- Do not take notes or worry about remembering or recording.
- Choose to let go of your agenda and critical judgment.
- Listen deeply and continuously, maintaining a perspective without judgment, for a period of no less than eight minutes.
- Explore whether your listening partner will repeat this exercise by listening to you in the same way.

Identity Molecule

Compassion: *Identity Molecule*

The Identity Molecule offers a profound practice to help you understand how others see their identity and share your sense of identity with others. Awareness and understanding of identity open pathways to deeper exploration of assumptions, beliefs, theories, worldviews, and their related underlying values and interests. A dialogue about identity with others opens pathways to compassion and collaboration.

The Molecule refers to the concept that our individual identities are constructed from our sense of belonging and participating in multiple, sometimes overlapping, groups that together form the individual Identity Molecule. In this way, identity evolves over time as group membership and affiliation arise, strengthen or recede.

The Identity Molecule is practiced with two or more individuals. This practice asks each person to identify five groups that express personal identity and explain how membership within each group developed and shaped a sense of self. The groups can then be numbered in order of centrality or importance to the individual's identity.

Step by Step

- Ask your dialogue partner what groups he or she feels part of that express his or her identity. Note that there is no right answer or approach to this question. The purpose of the inquiry is simply to understand how your partner conceives of his or her identity. You may be surprised by the many ways in which people think about their identity, in terms of gender, economics, geography, ethnicity, skin color, age, profession, language, sexual orientation and many other classifications.

- For each group identified, inquire about the genesis, history and meaning involved in belonging or conceiving of identity in terms of this group. How did membership come about? How has it evolved over time? What does the future hold? What does it mean?
- Ask your partner to order the groups by centrality and strength with reference to his or her current sense of identity. Have these priorities evolved over time? Is there a group that is getting stronger or one that is receding?
- As you return to this conversation over time, pay attention to how your partner's sense of identity is changing and evolving.

The Left Hand

Compassion: *The Left-Hand Column*

The Left-Hand Column describes the practice of being aware of those times in dialogue when you do not say what you are thinking. The practice is to imagine yourself writing down the exchange. What is said out loud goes in the right-hand column, while what remains thought but not spoken is written on the left-hand side. This practice also calls for you to be aware of when others may be engaging in the same behavior: not saying what they are really thinking. The goal of the practice is not to pass judgment on yourself or others, but to become aware of the breakdown in communications. Importantly, the goal is not necessarily to say out loud what you are thinking but not saying, but to observe the context for the omission and reflect upon it. Why do you, or why does someone else, choose not to express internal thoughts? What is gained and what is lost when these thoughts or feelings remain latent or obscured in some way?

Step by Step

- When in conversation, take note of the fact that there are some observations, feelings or other thoughts that are in your awareness but that you choose not to disclose.
- Notice what you are saying out loud in the conversation and imagine that this communication is printed in the right-hand column of a page with two columns.
- Notice what you are choosing not to express and imagine that this uncommunicated content is printed in the left-hand column of the same page.
- Ask yourself why you chose not to communicate what was in your left-hand column. What did you gain from keeping this unexpressed? What did you lose?

- Using your intuition, try to become aware of circumstances when others may not be expressing observations, thoughts or feelings during a conversation with you.
- The goal of this practice is not necessarily to share what is in the left-hand column. It is rather to be mindful of what is there, to understand why it is there, and to understand the costs and benefits of leaving this content unexpressed within the conversation.

Compassion

Compassion: *Compassion Meditation*

The Compassion Meditation practice offers a simple but powerful way for you to increase your compassionate engagement with others. The first step in Compassion Meditation is to visualize people for whom you feel very strong love, warmth, connection, solidarity, brotherhood or sisterhood. These could include lovers, family members, close friends or anyone who inspires such feelings. Those you visualize do not have to be currently living. They could be anyone from any part of your life who inspired you to feel a deep sense of compassion.

The next step in Compassion Meditation is to imagine several people whom you don't know very well, and try to extend your feelings of compassion to them.

Then visualize several strangers, people whom you barely know at all, and try to extend your feelings of compassion to them.

Next, visualize people toward whom you may feel anger, frustration or bitterness and try to extend your feelings of compassion toward them.

It is normal to experience resistance or difficulty in the effort to express compassion toward acquaintances, strangers or people toward whom you have negative feelings. The point is to use this practice to strengthen your compassion muscle.

Finally, envision yourself and direct your compassion toward your own body, mind and spirit.

As with all of the practices, do not become stuck intellectualizing or justifying this practice within a philosophy or religious tradition.

Step by Step

- Imagine being physically close to someone for whom you feel strong, mutual compassion. Imagine that you are holding his or her hands, sharing a meal together, sharing an embrace, or sharing eye contact in a supportive and loving way.
- Imagine the feelings and energy that you feel with this person.
- Now imagine someone who is merely an acquaintance. You know this person but don't feel a sense of intimacy or closeness. Imagine extending your feelings of compassion toward this person.
- Now imagine a stranger, someone whom you don't know, whom you may be meeting for the very first time. Imagine extending your feelings of compassion toward this person.
- Now imagine someone whom you dislike or perceive to be an enemy, someone who is a rival or whom you believe may be hostile to your success or well-being. Imagine extending your feelings of compassion toward this person.
- Now imagine yourself, your mind, your physical body, your spirit or soul, and extending compassion toward yourself.

Giving and Taking

Compassion: *Tonglen*

Tonglen (the name comes from the Tibetan word meaning "giving and taking") is practiced when you feel pain or any negative emotion or sensation arising within yourself or someone in your presence or awareness. We may be conditioned to resist, deny or react in some way against negative feelings or emotions. In Tonglen practice, we allow ourselves to take them in, metaphorically breathing in, touching or in any other way sensing what we experience as hot, painful, sore or in some way difficult or unpleasant. Then we summon up positive, compassionate, cool, nurturing, healing, peaceful emotions or sensations and metaphorically breathe them out as our response. Tonglen is a way of engaging what is painful, angry or difficult with a response that is benevolent, peaceful, healthful and healing. The power of Tonglen practice is to meet difficulty with peaceful, healing relief rather than escalating negative situations. You can practice this for yourself, others close to you who are suffering, or anyone who is suffering within your extended awareness. In this way, you are able to strengthen your ability to meet your own suffering and that of others with courage and benevolence.

Step by Step
- Notice the pain, discomfort or suffering that you or someone else may be experiencing.
- Open your mind and heart to experiencing the pain, discomfort or suffering. This may require strength and courage.
- Allow yourself to take in the difficult or negative emotions or sensations. Imagine that you are holding them within a container of energy inside your own mind and heart.

- Now convert the pain, discomfort, suffering or other negative emotions to peaceful, loving, healing energy.
- Breathe out, returning this positive energy to yourself or the person who is in discomfort or suffering.

The Celtic Spiral of Energy

Second Domain: Aspiring

Nothing can dim the light that shines from within.

Maya Angelou

The Second Domain

The Second Domain, Aspiring, involves three practices: Vision, Willpower and Resilience.

Vision practices involve imagining in great detail what you desire and want to create with others, yielding a powerful living picture of your chosen future.

Willpower practices increase your ability to focus energy on moving and shaping your current reality so that it comes into congruence with your vision.

Resilience practices help you learn from and persist in the face of obstacles and failures. The practices within the Aspiring Domain build your power as a collaborative creator. You are able to see what you want to create, take intentional actions toward manifesting this creation in reality, and transform obstacles and setbacks into learning and energy that enable you to realize your desires and goals while working closely with others.

Vision
Vision practices include two sub-practices:

- Journaling Your Vision and Values
- Connecting and Reconnecting with Your Vision and Values

These practices engage you in an intentional and thorough process of imagining in detail your dreams for yourself and others for whom you care. They also provide a path to connect on a daily and weekly basis with your aspirations so that they remain vital and evolve into the future.

Journaling is a practice that you undertake at least once a week. Connecting and Reconnecting with Your Vision and Values is a daily practice.

Willpower

Willpower practices include two sub-practices:

- Personal Visualization
- Surfing the Urge

Through the Personal Visualization sub-practice, you develop the ability to visualize specific daily actions to take and those to avoid that will lead you toward specific, measurable goals and objectives to create for yourself and others (your vision).

Through the sub-practice of Surfing the Urge, you strengthen your ability to stay focused on what you are creating without suffering from unhelpful distractions that may arise from primal feelings and impulses. These sub-practices are simple to describe yet they take much work to master. They translate into extraordinary willpower to help you manifest your vision through specific daily actions and self-control strategies.

Resilience

Within the Domain of Aspiring, Resilience sub-practices include:

- Pause and Plan
- Self-Forgiveness, Gratitude and Self-Care

Through the Pause and Plan sub-practice, you develop the ability to activate mindfulness, vision and willpower when you experience high levels of impulsiveness or difficult emotions driven by frustrations, setbacks, failures and other challenges within your creative engagement.

Through Self-Forgiveness, Gratitude and Self-Care, you develop the ability to activate self-compassion and compassion for others experiencing similar challenges involving intense feelings, emotions and impulses that may arise as a result of your engagement and aspiration. You are able to heal yourself, become stronger and increase endurance, while enhancing your energy as you move toward your creative visions.

Through these Resilience sub-practices, you become stronger under stress rather than experiencing burnout and diminishing effectiveness. You conduct these practices each day and as necessary when the situations require.

Journaling

Vision: *Journaling Your Vision and Values*

In this practice, you will examine your life through a series of focal areas such as spiritual development, physical and psychological health, your most important relationships, creativity, financial resources and your immediate surroundings (such as your home and community). You may add as many other focal areas as you wish according to your culture and values. The Domains of your Vision are really up to you to define.

Write a description of what you want to create in your life within each focal area in your journal at least once a week. Don't worry about whether your vision is practical, possible or feasible. This practice requires you to dream in an unconstrained way about what you truly desire for your life and for those with whom you are in relationships.

As you describe your visions, reflect upon your fundamental values: What do you care about in your life and why? Writing down your visions and values is a powerful practice that engages you in a dialogue with yourself about the future you want to create. This practice helps you to develop the belief that you can create, shape and improve your life, which is called a growth mindset.

Step by Step

- Select three to five focal areas that have a strong meaning to you as you think about your future. Examples are health, family, career, faith and community.
- Select a medium for your journal that you can always access. This could be a notebook that you keep with you, or an online space you can easily access.

- Select a time of the week when you have peace and privacy and at least one hour to write in your journal.
- Within each focal area, write down your thoughts about these questions: What do you want to create? Why and toward what end? How are you doing so far? What values underlie your creative visions for yourself? Be fearlessly honest with yourself. Try to explore your deepest and most passionate visions for your life.
- Return each week to build upon your reflections about these questions.

The Compass

Visioning: *Connecting and Reconnecting with Your Vision and Values*

In this practice, you take a moment each day to connect with your fundamental visions and values. Personalize this practice in a way that you find most effective. One suggestion is to employ active imagery.

Visualize an image that dynamically represents your vision within each focal Domain. For instance, if you cherish good health, imagine yourself engaged in activities that will strengthen and improve your health, such as hiking along a beautiful mountain trail, swimming in a clear lake or sitting down to a plate of fresh salad. Or imagine yourself in a state of joy sharing a meal or taking a walk with someone with whom you envision yourself in a positive relationship. In the area of spiritual development, imagine yourself in a place of great beauty experiencing wisdom or inner peace. As part of this practice, keep a card within easy reach on which you have written words or phrases that express your core vision and values as you have defined them in your journal. In this way, as you confront challenges, you can energize yourself, connecting with these images as a way to positively orient your thoughts and actions.

Step by Step

- Read through your journal of vision and values.
- In each focal area, create a dynamic mental image that captures the essence of your vision and values.
- Write down a short phrase that helps call to mind the mental image you have for each focal area on a card.
- Every day, upon waking or while going through your morning routine, look at the card or cards that you have created and call each image to mind as a reinforcement of your vision and values.

Celtic Awen, Symbol of Three Domains of Action

Willpower: *Personal Visualization, I Want, I Will, I Won't*

The visualization called for in this practice involves imagining something *you want* that is deeply connected to your overall vision, something that *you will* commit to do in the service of your vision and something that *you won't* do—in other words, an action that might interfere with your vision that you intentionally choose to avoid. Try to focus on your three most important areas of creative focus within each Domain of Visualization.

Use the "I Want" practice to visualize clear and specific achievements that would manifest your creative visions. Examples: I want to achieve a healthy body weight; I want to complete my degree; I want to finish writing my book.

Use the "I Will" practice to visualize yourself taking specific actions on the day of your visualization. Examples: I will exercise; I will eat healthy food; I will communicate love to someone about whom I care.

Use the "I Won't" practice to visualize yourself avoiding specific actions that you have decided not to undertake. Examples: I won't smoke any cigarettes today; I won't eat unhealthy foods; I won't absorb hateful speech from the media; I won't allow negative experiences to undermine my confidence.

Keep in mind that for the purpose of this practice, *visualizing* is distinct from *visioning*. Visualization involves actively imagining one or more specific scenarios that directly lead you toward your vision. So, if your vision involves reaching the summit of a mountain, you might visualize yourself climbing successfully throughout the day, not losing energy nor sustaining any injuries. If your vision involves writing a best-selling novel, you might visualize writing a riveting scene or developing a compelling character.

Imagine that your vision is to build a successful business. Your "I Want" visualization might involve wanting to create a strong team. *I want to create a strong team.* Your "I Will" visualization might involve searching for the best candidates. *I will find the best available team members.* Your "I Won't" visualization might involve committing not to settle for less than that required for excellence. *I won't settle for second best.*

Another example may be your vision to build a strong relationship with your spouse or significant other. The visualization for this would be: *I want to build a loving relationship infused with trust and mutual support. I will verbally and through my actions consistently express my love and thoughtfulness. I will not be short-tempered or self-centered.*

Set aside a short period of time to engage in this visualization practice for all of the visions that you have for yourself. The practice will help you to undertake specific actions and behaviors to support your visions and to avoid those that could slow your progress.

This can be combined with the Connecting and Reconnecting with Your Visions and Values practice to orient your vision and values with respect to specific courses of action that give them life and reality.

Step by Step

- Select a focal area of your life, for example health, family or career.
- Determine a specific achievement that will directly lead to realizing your vision in this area.
- Describe the achievement in a short phrase.
- Now write down: "I want..." and add that phrase associated with this specific achievement.
- Determine a specific action to take that will directly lead to this achievement.
- Describe this action in a short phrase.
- Now write down, "I will..." and add that phrase associated with this specific action.
- Determine a specific action or behavior that could undermine or frustrate your ability to undertake your vision or its related achievement.
- Describe this unhelpful action or behavior in a short phrase.

- Now write down, "I won't..." and add that phrase associated with this unhelpful action or behavior.
- Now read and remember all three commitments related to your vision. "I want—I will—I won't—."
- Review your statements at the start of each day when you connect with your vision and values.
- As you accomplish key achievements and move toward your most fundamental visions, allow your commitments to evolve accordingly.
- Repeat this practice for at least three of your most important focal areas of vision.

Waves

Willpower: *Self-Mastery—Surfing the Urge*

Surfing the Urge is a practice that combines observing your impulsive mind with the practice of Tonglen (p. 19).

This practice begins with developing a sensitive, alert mindfulness about your basic desires and urges, many of which flow from your primal self. These can sometimes be observed in volatile emotions such as anger, fear, pleasure and desire.

This practice has three parts. First, you must notice and be mindful of the urge before acting on it. Learn to notice hunger, anger, fear, longing and desire as these powerful feelings are beginning to take hold, the way you might notice a distant ocean wave making its way to the shoreline.

Second, rather than sit in denial of the urge or in opposition to it, be mindful of it. Allow yourself to experience the urge or feeling. Allow it to wash over you. You can experience this process of taking in the urge or feeling as if you were taking a deep inward breath and then letting it go, passing through and away from you.

You may find that the Domain of Aspiring often leads you to feel frustrated. You might feel a temptation to give up or to take self-defeating actions that work against your vision. If your vision is to climb a mountain summit, you may feel tempted to give up and walk downhill given its difficulty, or take a risky shortcut to save time and energy. You might lose focus and be tempted to daydream about something more comforting than the arduous work of climbing.

This practice calls upon you to pay attention to these feelings and to fully experience them. This is accompanied by a deep, reflective, inward breath. Allow the feelings to wash over you: temptation, the urge toward distraction and/or self-defeating behaviors. Then surf these feelings and breathe out, allowing them to roll over and past you, remaining strong in your vision and visualization. Fully feel your urges and emotions using mindfulness techniques, but do not allow yourself to go under or be washed away by emotions or temptations.

Imagine that your vision is to attain optimal health. Visualize yourself avoiding sugary foods and, at a social gathering, you see a tempting dessert loaded with sugar. Take a deep breath and allow yourself to fully feel your desire and the temptation to consume the dessert. You allow the urge to pass, surfing through it. Then you return to your vision and visualization. *I won't eat sugary foods.*

Step by Step

- Observe feelings, emotions and urges as they begin to form.
- Breathe in deeply, allowing them to become fully manifest and present in your mind and heart. (This is the opposite of denying or frustrating your emotional state. For example, as anger rises up, fully observe: "I am feeling very angry.")
- Breathe out, allowing the feeling, urge or emotion to wash over and then away from you.
- Call to mind your vision, values and commitments.
- Act patiently and wisely in a way that leads toward your most deeply held visions and values.

Finding the Path

Resilience: *Pause and Plan*

Working in the Domains of Engaging and Aspiring necessarily gives rise to challenges and strong related emotions, which arise when you observe the divergence between reality and your creative visions. At such times, we may encounter forces that seem, at best, disinterested or uncaring about our aspirations and, at worst, opposing or even hostile to our dreams, goals and sense of well-being. During such experiences, we may be tempted to lash out in pain or anger, become reactive, fight back or flee in a quest for respite, safety or relief from stress. A healthier practice is to consciously slow down, summon our highest awareness and enter into a concentrated, courageous, deliberative and thoughtful state of mind.

If you slow down, pause and awaken your highest consciousness, choosing to act deliberately and thoughtfully rather than reflexively, you will move more steadily toward your visions and aspirations. The Pause practice draws on your ability to "surf the urge." Take a moment to observe and fully comprehend your reactive, emotional state in the face of discomfort, frustration or other challenges. The Plan practice comes when you draw deeply upon your value-based visions, reflecting upon long-range (rather than short-term) dynamics. If you have patience, what wise actions will lead most efficiently to your aspirations in a way that fully reflect your values? You must awaken and engage your higher consciousness to summon this Plan practice.

Imagine that you are working to improve an important relationship. This could involve relations with a close family member, colleague or client. As you are working on the relationship, a crisis occurs and you experience a severe conflict with this person, leading to bitterness and anger.

At this point you might be tempted to abandon this person and avoid further encounters. While feeling hot, painful or frustrating emotions, you might decide, "That's it! I am *done* with this person." But within the Pause and Plan practice, you could decide to approach this situation differently.

Pausing allows you to surf the urge and Planning will allow you to re-connect with your vision, values and visualizations. You may come to the same conclusion—that you need to move on from the relationship caus-ing discomfort. But your final decision and approach will be made em-ploying your highest consciousness and best wisdom, rather than being undertaken as an emotional reaction. You do not disregard your emo-tions; rather, you allow yourself to fully feel and understand them while separating them from immediate action. The Pause and Plan practice al-lows you to show resilience in managing a difficult situation, and may ex-pose other options and possibilities that lead you toward the realization of your deepest aspirations.

Step by Step

- In response to any situation that creates feelings of stress, anger, pain, fear, resentment or other difficult emotions, intentionally step back. Take a timeout and intentionally pause. During this time, employ the practice of Surfing the Urge.
- In order to plan, reconnect with your visions, values and visualizations in terms of "*I want, I will, I won't.*"
- In order to plan, call to mind the dynamic variables associated with your visions and notice to what extent this situation affects or influences them.
- Act patiently and wisely in a way that leads toward your most deeply held visions and values.

Hands Make Heart

Resilience: *Self-Forgiveness, Gratitude and Self-Care*

As you undertake the practices involved in Engaging, Aspiring and Achieving, you will repeatedly experience failures and shortcomings. There may arise within you a tendency to begin to dwell upon your past failures and shortcomings and to worry about future problems. Through the practice of self-forgiveness and self-care, you learn from the past but do not dwell upon it or fear repeating shortcomings. You show yourself compassion, understanding and positive regard, with courage and confidence for the future. Give courage and confidence to yourself as a loving gift, without concern for how you or others perceive or judge your past performances.

Understand that you are the vessel for the loving compassion of the infinite spirit, your own inward sun. In this Resilience practice, you learn from the past but then let it go and reside fully in the present moment, gaining courage, concentration and self-compassion from your sun. To experience gratitude is an essential component of this practice. Experience joy and solace by reflecting on the simple beauties and pleasures that abound around us and that we can appreciate through connection to our own spirit.

Step by Step
- Call to mind all of the people, relationships, and gifts that support you and your life.
- Reflect on your relationship with the infinite spirit, the inward sun, that animates your own soul. Feel the compassionate presence of this spirit supporting you.

- Mindfully observe and embrace your personal failures and shortcomings. Allow them to become fully present in your mind and heart.
- Ask yourself what you can learn from your failures and shortcomings. What gifts do your past experiences offer you? How can you benefit from your past experiences in the future?
- Fully commit yourself to carrying your learning from past experiences into the future so as to grow stronger and move toward your visions and values more swiftly and with certainty.
- Exercising self-compassion, generously forgive yourself for your past failures and shortcomings, letting them go with a sense of humility and good humor.
- Choose to live in the present rather than the past.
- Reconnect with your visions, values and visualizations, with confidence and courage about your ability to learn, grow and achieve.

The Celtic Triskelion

Third Domain: Achieving

The love within us is meant to extend outward. The closer we grow to our inner light, we feel a natural urge to share it. We all long for meaningful work, some creative endeavor that will be our ministry, by which the energies within us might flow out to help heal the world.

Marianne Williamson

The Third Domain

The Third Domain, Achieving, involves two practices: Dynamics and Genership (Collaborative Creativity). Dynamics takes up elements of the practice of systems thinking, which helps you to understand yourself, others and the world around you in terms of dynamic, interrelated changes. Through increased mindfulness about change, you are able to enhance your creative power in collaboration with others by identifying and acting upon aspects of yourself and your environment that can change and are subject to your intentional influence. This practice also allows you to engage and harness extended networks of change to influence areas that may be removed from your immediate span of influence.

Ambitious change initiatives require this ability to harness complex systems. In turn, through Genership, you develop the ability to collaborate effectively with others in such change initiatives, increasing your power through effective teams and organizations, thereby mastering group creativity.

Dynamics

Dynamics involves three sub-practices:

- Courage, Concentration and Peak Performance
- Framing Visions and Values as Dynamic Variables
- Observing Dynamic Relationships Between Variables Related to Visions and Values

Through the sub-practice of Courage, Concentration and Peak Performance, we form a bridge from resilience to achievement. This allows us to focus and continue our change practices within stressful situations where our impulses or emotions may create unwanted distractions that divert or frustrate our attention or energy.

Through the sub-practice of Framing Visions and Values as Dynamic Variables, we begin to navigate creatively within environments that may be subject to rapid and complex change.

Through the sub-practice of Observing Dynamic Relationships Between Variables Related to Visions and Values, we begin to work with others to harness dynamic systems effectively, gaining the power to manifest changes using energy and cascading changes available within extended systems.

When combined, these three sub-practices enable a quantum leap in our creative power, accelerating our ability to manifest ambitious visions in reality.

Courage, Concentration and Peak Performance is a practice that you conduct as needed. Conduct Framing Vision and Values as Dynamic Variables at least on a weekly basis. Conduct the practice of Observing Dynamic Relationships Between Variables Related to Visions and Values on a daily basis.

Genership

Genership involves four sub-practices:

- Surfacing Mental Models, Interests and Visions
- Seeking Help for Our Interests and Visions
- Benevolent, Constructive Engagement
- Collaborative Participation in Circles of Practice

The sub-practice of Surfacing Mental Models, Interests and Visions allows us to radically deepen our collaborative efficacy. Through this practice, we become mindful of how others see us and their world and understand their creative desires, goals and objectives with increased awareness that exposes new potential for collaboration.

Through the sub-practice of Seeking Help for Our Interests and Visions, we increase our creative power by opening up our own creative aspirations to evolution and assistance from others. We benefit from their compassionate energy directed toward our creative work.

The sub-practice of Benevolent, Constructive Engagement reinforces this collaborative benefit and increases our own compassionate engagement in assisting others with their projects. In this way, we begin to develop synergy among effective collaborations and experience the creative feedback that accelerates as our creative visions evolve and manifest in concert with those of others.

Finally, through the sub-practice of Collaborative Participation in Circles of Practice, we work together to deepen and evolve our own practices, thereby strengthening ourselves and those with whom we are collaborating. We grow stronger, more resilient and effective, and experience increased energy over time. With the exception of Collaborative Participation in Circles of Practice, you conduct all of these sub-practices with others every day, and Circles of Practice at least once a month.

Thunderbird

Dynamics: *Courage, Concentration and Peak Performance*

Through the practice of Courage, Concentration and Peak Performance, you form a bridge from resilience to achievement and have access to your best self and greatest powers during your toughest, most difficult moments. Stress doesn't have to weaken you; with self-awareness, it makes you stronger!

The Courage element of this practice involves your ability to draw strength from your most deeply held visions and values during periods of high stress and volatile emotions. You turn inward to draw on the infinite inner powers that reside in the deepest reserves of your spiritual center. You find the connection between your individual life and the universe itself.

The Concentration element of this practice involves channeling all of your spiritual energy into the current moment without being distracted or dissipated by fear, worry or doubt arising from the past or future. Your Mindfulness Meditation practice will help increase your ability to concentrate.

Peak Performance practice involves learning to habitually respond to pressure and stress with your most powerful and skillful effort. It is the practice of being fully present and marshalling your best abilities under the most difficult circumstances.

Step by Step

- Mindfully observe the situation or task before you, becoming fully conscious of the demands it will place on your mind, body and spirit.
- Fully reconnect with your vision, values and visualizations as they relate to this situation or task.

41

- Make a specific visualization about this situation or task: *I want to realize my visions and live out my values; I will give this situation my deepest and fullest attention, confidently delivering all of my abilities and skills, and realizing my peak performance; I won't allow myself to be distracted by uncertainty, fear, doubt or worry.*
- Dive in and deliver your peak performance, fully focusing yourself on the actions at hand without distraction or concern over failure or falling short.
- Fully sustain your peak performance through to completion.

Delta (Change)

Dynamics: *Framing Visions and Values as Dynamic Variables*

This practice entails thoughtful exploration and analysis of your visions and values, interpreting and visualizing them in terms of changeable factors within your span of control or influence.

Suppose your vision involves attaining spiritual enlightenment. You might reflect on the concept that this may arise from an increasing investment of time in meditation and contemplation. This time investment can be within your span of control, and you can decide to increase such time invested.

In a different arena, suppose that your vision is to attain the level of physical fitness where you can enjoy a hike of many miles in rough, mountainous terrain. Upon reflection, you determine that your ability to achieve your vision is determined by at least three critical variables: your body weight, the strength and endurance of your feet, legs and core, and your level of cardiovascular fitness. These are all subject to your control. You can decide to restrict your diet, eat healthy foods and begin an exercise regimen. Over time, your weight can be reduced; with exercise, your feet, legs and core can strengthen; and your cardiovascular fitness will improve. Your control over these variables allows you to achieve your vision.

Take the value of integrity. With reflection, you define this as your level of honesty and ability to follow through on your commitments. You begin to observe the extent to which you are honest in your communications with others, striving in each to increase your level of honesty. This effort to frame the generalized value of integrity with specificity as your level of honesty in ongoing interpersonal communications provides a clear pathway to realize your values in practice.

Step by Step

- Within your journal of visions and values, select a focal area for this practice.
- Take this focal area and reflect upon what factors would need to change in you and your environment for you to realize your vision and values.
- Frame these factors that would need to change as one or more coherent, measurable variables that you can influence through your immediate actions and behaviors.
- List these variables within your journal.
- On a weekly basis, reflect upon and refine your framing of these variables in a way that makes them increasingly tangible, measurable and accessible to your immediate influence.
- Repeat this process for each focal area within your journal of visions and values.

Systems Thinking

Dynamics: *Observing Dynamic Relationships Connected to Visions and Values*

This practice involves exploring the system of relationships between the key variables within your span of influence. Understanding these relationships allows you to focus on variables that have high levels of influence over others that you may also wish to influence, and to harness helpful systemic feedback and avoid counterproductive feedback.

This practice is the essence of all systems wisdom: how to make change effectively and efficiently without backsliding or setting off unintended negative consequences. Increasing mindfulness, as an example, increases awareness, concentration and self-control, thereby creating positive feedback that leads in a loop to further increases in mindfulness. On the other hand, if you were to respond to stress by taking drugs that create a temporary feeling of euphoria, but which also undermine your perception of reality, this may have unintended consequences. You might create more stress that arises from your inability to assess and respond to important changes in reality.

Imagine that you want to increase your cardiovascular health. You reduce your eating and increase your exercise. Doing this, you lose weight, allowing you to further increase your exercise, which further reduces your weight. As you spend more time exercising, you spend less time eating, and this further reduces your weight. As you lose weight, you are healthier, and this creates more avenues for exercise, further reducing your weight and further strengthening your cardiovascular health.

Such examples abound in all fields of aspiration and endeavor. Mastery of our creative process requires that we explore the connections and relationships among the variables that we frame, constantly testing and evaluating how they influence one another.

Step by Step

- Explore the relationships between and among the dynamic variables that define your vision and values.
- Look for reinforcing connections. These are relationships that move the variables in the same direction, meaning when one variable increases, it causes the other to increase, and when one decreases, it causes the other to do so also. Explore whether the sequence matters. For example, eating less food may cause you to lose weight, but losing weight does not necessarily cause you to eat less food. Increasing time studying information may cause your understanding to increase, but increasing your understanding does not necessarily increase your time spent studying.
- Look for balancing, counteracting connections. These are relationships that move variables in opposite directions, meaning that when one increases, the other decreases and vice versa. Again, explore whether the sequence matters. As your hunger increases, your eating activity will eventually go up, but as your eating activity increases, your hunger will decrease.
- Test employing the relationships among connected variables to create positive, reinforcing system dynamics that lead toward your visions and values. This will happen through patterns of reinforcing and counteracting connections that you intentionally influence.

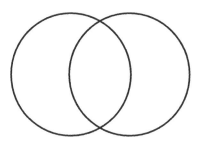

Exploring Mental Models

Genership: *Surfacing Mental Models, Interests and Visions*

This practice involves intentionally developing a Domain of dialogue that increases consciousness in three important areas.

First, we must develop consciousness of the assumptions, beliefs and worldviews that influence how we understand reality, and how those with whom we interact understand it. How do we and others conceive of our own identity and purpose? What do we and others believe to be true? How are our beliefs and those of others shaped and tested? How does all of this affect how we understand what we see and express to one another? This Domain—the mental lenses through which we perceive the world and our communications with one another—is called Mental Models.

Second, we must develop consciousness of our interests and those of others. Interests include values, desires, goals and immediate objectives. What do we want for ourselves and others, and what do they want for us?

Third, we must develop consciousness of our own broad visions and those of others. In the widest perspective, what are we and others working to create in the future and toward what ends? This sub-practice requires us to compare and contrast our mental models, interests and visions with those held by others and gain mutual understanding about the similarities and differences. We must practice doing this without becoming mired in judgment and conflict. This practice is critical because without such an open exploration, we may fail to understand our respective communications or to assist one another in collaborations. We may also unintentionally thwart one another's progress.

Step by Step

- Identify the key individuals in your environment with whom you are in existing or potential relationships or collaborations. These could be acquaintances, friends, family members, work or professional colleagues, or the community at large.
- Within such interactions, make it a point to open dialogue that explores their assumptions, beliefs, theories, worldviews and experiences that shape their perceptions.
- Then expand your dialogue to include understanding their values, desires, goals and immediate objectives. Share your own in the same way.
- Next, expand your dialogue to include a deep understanding of their long-range visions for themselves and others. Share your own long-range visions as well.
- Finally, take in and explore areas of similarity, difference and tension regarding the above subjects of dialogue.

Open Circle with Intention

Genership: *Seeking Help for Our Visions and Interests*

This practice requires us to be vocal with everyone in our circle, mindfully expressing our broadest visions and related, more immediate interests: our values, desires, goals and objectives. We must practice helping others to understand what we are attempting to create in the world and then asking for their active support. This is the beginning of all meaningful collaboration and co-creative efforts, requiring us to have the courage to receive and work through questions, challenges and negative feedback about our visions and interests. In this regard, we may have to resort to other practices, including Tonglen and Surfing the Urge. When we make a practice of expressing our visions and interests, we open up pathways for others to help us with information, collaboration and compassion. Over time, the positive energy that we receive will overwhelm the negative energy. Importantly, when we engage in creative, constructive dialogue with others, our aspirations and efforts will evolve and grow stronger. And when we successfully navigate challenges and even attempts to thwart our aspirations, we will inevitably become stronger and more resilient.

Step by Step

- Identify the key individuals in your environment with whom you are in existing or potential relationships or collaborations. These could be among acquaintances, friends, family members, work or professional colleagues, or the community at large.
- Within your interactions with these individuals, make it a point to open dialogue in which you share *your* values, desires, goals and objectives.
- Share *your* long-range visions for yourself and others.

- Intentionally ask others to help you by providing information and ideas, and to take action to help you live out *your* values and achieve your desires, goals and objectives.
- Practice Surfing the Urge, Tonglen, Pause and Plan, and Systems Wisdom as others give you feedback and assistance.

Benevolent, Constructive Engagement

Genership: *Benevolent, Constructive Engagement*

This practice involves demonstrating constructive goodwill toward others and offering our assistance. We work to understand and help others satisfy their interests in pursuit of their value-based visions. Such benevolent and constructive relations build powerful networks of support that in turn support our own visions and interests. Benevolence is achieved through compassionate, forgiving, positive energy directed toward those we encounter in an effort to relieve their suffering, increase their knowledge and capacity, and contribute to their success. Constructive Engagement means finding specific, tangible and sincere offers of meaningful support that can be experienced and measured by those who receive it.

Step by Step

- Identify the key individuals in your environment with whom you are in existing or potential relationships or collaborations. These could be among acquaintances, friends, family members, work or professional colleagues, or the community at large.
- Within your interactions with these individuals, make it a point to open dialogue in which you understand *their* values, desires, goals and objectives.
- Open dialogue in which you understand *their* long-range visions for themselves and others.
- In areas consistent with your values, help others by providing information and ideas that could assist them.
- In areas consistent with your values, take action to help others live out *their* values and achieve *their* desires, goals and objectives.
- Practice Surfing the Urge, Tonglen, Pause and Plan, and Systems Wisdom as you give others feedback and assistance.

Circles of Practice

Genership: *Collaborative Participation in Circles of Practice*

This practice involves joining with others benevolently and construc-
tively to share the practices outlined above that are comprised within the
themes of engagement, aspiration and achievement. This practice recog-
nizes that the compassion generated within such circles of practice can
be a powerful resource in mastering and evolving the practices.

Step by Step

- Join our national community of practice via the I-LEAD Society at
  www.i-lead.social.
- Join an online practice circle or find a local circle where you can meet
  in person.
- Read the articles and books available through our national
  community of practice.
- Attend biweekly online practice sessions that focus collaboratively on
  strengthening your skills and abilities.
- Meet with fellow practitioners locally and expand your network.
- Attend one of our local conferences for practitioners.
- This is a living community, so please contribute to our practice
  movement by expanding and evolving the base-camp practices
  through our online community. Share your experiments,
  experiences, breakthroughs and learnings.

Next Steps: From Base Camp to the Treeline

Anyone with mountain-climbing experience knows about the treeline: the place at higher altitudes where trees no longer grow. As you climb out of base camp, trees are beautiful and provide shelter. But they also limit visibility. When you rise above the treeline, the vistas open. You may be able to see the summit for the first time. You have a sense of how far you have traveled. A transition takes place both in the environment and for you, as a climber. You have a sense of accomplishment combined with a sense of wonder and excitement about the challenges that lie before you.

The practices outlined throughout this book will help you get to this extraordinary place where the vistas open. You will have a sense of having grown stronger, of the reality that new challenges and possibilities are ahead. The practices that lead from base camp to the treeline promise a soul-fulfilling journey filled with meaning. They are part of the path that leads to your unique destiny.

How should you go about implementing the baseline practices? There is ultimately no right answer to this question, only your own experimentation to find out what works for you. We can, however, offer some guidelines based on our personal experience. Some practices work well on a daily basis. Some benefit from more time between practice sessions. These can be implemented weekly. Some activities require others to join you in the practice, and some you may want to keep closely at hand to use when situations demand.

The practices can be compared to a set of physical exercises. Some, like stretching or warming up, need to take place every day. Some are specialized, to develop certain sets of spiritual and psychological muscles. These benefit from being employed less frequently, with opportunities for rest, reflection and recovery. And just like some physical exercises, some practices require a partner.

Daily Practices on Your Own
Mindfulness Meditation
Compassion Meditation
Reconnecting with Visions and Values
Visualization: I Want, I Will, I Won't

Weekly Practices on Your Own
Journaling
Framing Vision and Values as Dynamic Variables

As Necessary on Your Own
Observe Your Impulsive Mind
Observe Your Stress Response
Surf the Urge
Tonglen (for Self)
Self-Forgiveness, Gratitude and Self-Care
Pause and Plan (Rather than Fight or Flight)
Observe Connections Among Key Variables
Courage, Confidence and Peak Performance

Daily Practices with Others
Tonglen
Left-Hand Column
Surfacing Mental Models, Interests and Visions
Expressing and Seeking Help for Our Interests and Visions
Unconditional, Benevolent and Constructive Engagement

Weekly Practices with Others
Listening (Eight Minutes)
Identity Molecule
Sharing in Circles of Practice with Others

Please join the I-LEAD Society

Our national community of practice is available on the web at www.i-lead. social. Within this online resource you will find local practice circles and additional published resources that you can use to learn more about the Seven Practices as well as links to articles and books that take you more deeply into the philosophical thought, ongoing research and experiential learning that supports this movement. These practices constitute a system of learning and action that is living and evolving as you read these words. We look forward to climbing together, and we will see you on the mountaintop!

About the Author: David M. Castro

In 1993, following a successful career both in private practice and as a Philadelphia prosecutor, Dave was awarded a Kellogg Foundation Leadership Program Fellowship, for which he studied leadership development and its relation to improving the quality of life in disadvantaged communities with Peter Senge (Center for Organizational Learning), Roger Fisher (Harvard Negotiation Project) and Don Clifton (the Gallup Organization). In 2002, Dave was awarded an Eisenhower Fellowship that he used to study leadership and its impact on economic and community development in Turkey. In 2009, he was named a Fellow by Ashoka, an international community of the world's leading social entrepreneurs.

As president and CEO of the Institute for Leadership Education, Advancement & Development (I-LEAD, Inc.), Dave is an accomplished leadership trainer and consultant with over 20 years of experience, including for major clients such as the Pennsylvania Commission on Crime and Delinquency, the U.S. Department of Agriculture, the Texas Department of Transportation, the W.K. Kellogg Foundation and Ashoka.

Dave's book, *Genership: Beyond Leadership Toward Liberating the Creative Soul,* is available in print and e-book formats. He is a graduate of Haverford College and the University of Pennsylvania Law School.

Made in the USA
Monee, IL
26 October 2020